March 29, 2010

Di

stories here that you
will enjoy,

with love,
Ruth

# Ruth....so far

by Ruth Pizzat

Copyright © 2010 by Ruth Pizzat
All rights reserved.

No part of this book may be reproduced or transmitted in any form or by any means electronic, or mechanical, including photocopying, recording or by any information storage and retrieval system, without permission in writing from the publisher. No abridgement or changes to the text are authorized by the publisher.

Original cover art, *Pink Square* and *Portrait Collage*, by Joseph Pizzat. Photos in *Portrait Collage* and cover photography by Corky Burt. Interior layout by David Russell.

ISBN number: 978-1-59712-404-1

Printed in the United States of America by
Catawba Publishing Company
First Printing

Order from
Catawba Publishing Company
(704) 717-8452
www.catawbapublishing.com

# Table of Contents

A Gift - An Introduction .................... xiii

## 1988
Feathers .................................. 1

## 1989
897- ...................................... 2
A Certitude ............................... 3
Birds of Paradise, The Painting ........... 4
Brontosaurus Lane ......................... 5
Commas for Dorothy ........................ 6
Good Morning .............................. 7
I Hadn't Planned To Love You .............. 8
Morning Exercise .......................... 9
Of Two Minds .............................. 10
Prescription Question ..................... 11
Shirley ................................... 12
The Professional .......................... 13
The Search ................................ 14
While ..................................... 15

## 1990
A Parting ................................. 16
Academic Genealogy ........................ 17
Yo, Brutus – A Letter to Amy .............. 18
Worry Train ............................... 19

## 1992
Joy ....................................... 20

## 1994
February Morning on Peach Street .......... 21
Your Song ................................. 22

**1995**
A Saint in Training .............................. 23
Sunday Mass .................................. 24

**1996**
*hurry* .......................................... 25
I'm Glad I Kissed Each Flower .................. 26
Late Spring Comes to the Peninsula ............. 27
Marriage Encounter– Encountered Too Often ..... 28
Not From the Portuguese Sonnets ............... 30
The Pig Iron Press ............................. 31
Who's Whose Self .............................. 32

**1997**
A Definition of God ............................ 33
Anna Freundel ................................. 34
April Snow .................................... 35
February 9 .................................... 36
Invisible ...................................... 37
PET Scan ..................................... 38
Roots ........................................ 39
Waiting for Laura ............................. 40

**1999**
Monday Visitors .............................. 41
My Mother and I .............................. 42
October ...................................... 43
View from My Window ........................ 45

**2000**
Bonnie's Car .................................. 46
Losers ........................................ 48
Lunch at the Club ............................. 49
Summer Vacation As Remembered by Joe ........ 52
The Best Love ................................. 53
Young Davids ................................. 54

**2001**
Attendance at Mass ........................... 55
E-mail ........................................ 56

Logos .......................................... 57
Nonny .......................................... 58
Sunday Morning Daughters .................... 59
The 22$^{nd}$ Day of Snow ........................... 60
The Universe Up Close ........................ 61
The Wind Blows Where It Will ................. 62
When You Grow Old ........................... 63

## 2002
Cry ............................................. 64
Gherkins ....................................... 65
Home .......................................... 66
It's Not Just Getting There .................... 68
Requiescat Bells .............................. 70
Requiescat Pacem ............................ 71
Supply Work ................................... 72
The Attack .................................... 73
The Women Next Door ........................ 74

## 2003
The Obit Page ................................. 75

## 2004
A Blanket of Birdsong ......................... 76
A Pickle ....................................... 77
Anxious Annie ................................ 78
Celebration in the Barnyard .................. 79
Little Gus ..................................... 80
My Friends .................................... 81
The Peacock .................................. 83

## 2005
Delfino ........................................ 84
His Passion ................................... 86
Litany for Philip .............................. 87
Prayer Place .................................. 88
Rehearsals .................................... 89
Seasons Greetings ............................ 90
What Color Is God ............................ 91

ix

## 2006

A Poem Is . . . . . . . . . . . . . . . . . . . . . . . . . . . . . . . . . 92
Be Careful . . . . . . . . . . . . . . . . . . . . . . . . . . . . . . . . 93
Clay Piece . . . . . . . . . . . . . . . . . . . . . . . . . . . . . . . . 94
Genealogy 101 . . . . . . . . . . . . . . . . . . . . . . . . . . . . . 95
I Did Not Believe . . . . . . . . . . . . . . . . . . . . . . . . . . . 96
Mr. and Mrs. Bentover . . . . . . . . . . . . . . . . . . . . . . . 97
No Empty Attics . . . . . . . . . . . . . . . . . . . . . . . . . . . 98
Patience . . . . . . . . . . . . . . . . . . . . . . . . . . . . . . . . . 99
Praise Song . . . . . . . . . . . . . . . . . . . . . . . . . . . . . . 100
The Word . . . . . . . . . . . . . . . . . . . . . . . . . . . . . . . 101

## 2007

Bruce . . . . . . . . . . . . . . . . . . . . . . . . . . . . . . . . . . 102
Church . . . . . . . . . . . . . . . . . . . . . . . . . . . . . . . . . 103
Dolly . . . . . . . . . . . . . . . . . . . . . . . . . . . . . . . . . . 104
Just Ask . . . . . . . . . . . . . . . . . . . . . . . . . . . . . . . . 113
Justice by Lena . . . . . . . . . . . . . . . . . . . . . . . . . . . 114
Lispeth's Birthday . . . . . . . . . . . . . . . . . . . . . . . . . 115
Not a Poem . . . . . . . . . . . . . . . . . . . . . . . . . . . . . 116
Not Writing . . . . . . . . . . . . . . . . . . . . . . . . . . . . . 117
Poem House . . . . . . . . . . . . . . . . . . . . . . . . . . . . 118
Scents of Life . . . . . . . . . . . . . . . . . . . . . . . . . . . . 119
The Eleventh McGriffin . . . . . . . . . . . . . . . . . . . . 120
Thickening . . . . . . . . . . . . . . . . . . . . . . . . . . . . . 121
Thursday Morning Walk . . . . . . . . . . . . . . . . . . . 122
When . . . . . . . . . . . . . . . . . . . . . . . . . . . . . . . . . 123
Where Have All the Old Girls Gone . . . . . . . . . . . . 124

## 2008

Again . . . . . . . . . . . . . . . . . . . . . . . . . . . . . . . . . 125
Car Gene . . . . . . . . . . . . . . . . . . . . . . . . . . . . . . 126
It Is The Season . . . . . . . . . . . . . . . . . . . . . . . . . 128
Limbo . . . . . . . . . . . . . . . . . . . . . . . . . . . . . . . . 130
The Doctors . . . . . . . . . . . . . . . . . . . . . . . . . . . . 131

## 2009

Cyrus Davis . . . . . . . . . . . . . . . . . . . . . . . . . . . . 132

Poems and stories previously published. . . . . . . . . . . 136

# A Gift - An Introduction

When I wakened in a Pittsburgh hospital the morning of June 29, 1988, I knew I was back. And I knew I had been away.

The day before, neurosurgeon Dr. Joseph Maroon had removed a massive, benign brain tumor that had destroyed my sense of smell, was growing around my right optic nerve and had impacted my thinking and behavior. My self had been taken away and I didn't know it. It took a number of months to realize the enormity that I had slowly become more and more lost over the past several years.

The surgery returned my life and my self.

Fortunately, I needed no further treatment beyond Dilantin for 15 months. My right eye recovered completely by the following spring. Since I was not allowed to drive, I was home much of that year.

I returned to my love for writing. A first poem, Feathers, was put down on paper a month after the surgery. This book is a compilation of poems and stories done from then until 2009. Most of them are printed as originally written.

It was a profound experience to have lost one's self and then regained it. Every day I am here I am grateful to be, to be me.

Ruth Pizzat

# [ 1988 ]

## Feathers

A wispy bunch of feathers
flies around my brain.
I can't remember Susan,
don't recall Elaine.
Or even Eldreth.
Eldreth?
The doctors say a month or two
all will be right as rain.
And I'll remember Susan,
recall all about Elaine.
But Eldreth?
Who's Eldreth?

## [ 1989 ]

### 897-

Sometimes
I start to dial your number.
Then I remember,
you're not there.

## A Certitude

I know,

God holds me by a string
that comes from heaven
to the top of my head
and makes my lightened feet

Dance!

## Birds Of Paradise, The Painting

Phoenix-like
they rise from frames of silver,
mats of beige and gray
into an escaping blue.

Winged birds
who just yesterday
were held fast in green of plant
and sea of sand.

Quickly, all new
they soar, reborn,
beyond a black Maui mountain
that cannot leave its molten feet.

Each takes its turn.
An endless rainbow of colors becomes color
when Paradise dips down
and lifts each fluttering unto itself.

# Brontosaurus Lane

Our Brontosaurus baby is banging down the lane.
It's coming, loud and snarling.
Its smoke is foul.
It spits and snorts.
It shakes the winter morning.

The air is split by cries and shouts.
There is no place for hiding.
It stops outside.
My sleep departs.
I rise to face the morning.

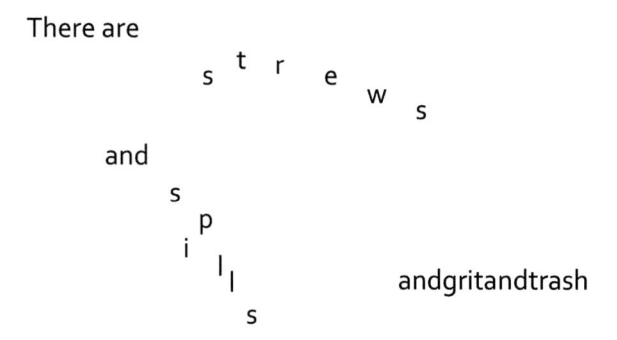

    There are
                s  <sup>t</sup>  <sup>r</sup>  e
                           w
                              s
      and
         s
           p
        i
         l
          l                   andgritandtrash
          s

But it has taken the weekly garbage.

## Commas for Dorothy

Thursday March 9, 1989

Dear Dorothy,

Enclosed are some commas for you you to use:

, ,' '      , ' , ' ,' '
 , '    ,  , ,    , ' , '
    , ' , ''      , ' , ' ,
       , ,     ,     , ,
        ,    ,    ,
(they spilled)                    ,
                                ,
I left one off at the end of the first line of the poem I sent.    ,

Please use the above on any copies you may make to send         '
to family or friend. If you have already sent any, guess you'll
just have to mail one in an envelope.                           ,

If you have any left, please don't bother to return them. They can be used as a semicolon if you can scarf up a period; few people use these anymore.

Or turn upside down and placed next-to-next they
make an acceptable quote
                  \ \
         or even an unquote



                      ' '
       ڔ                    ''
                     , ,
         if you can get them going the right direction

Anyway, my apologies for the oversight. Hope I've sent enough

                love,
                   *Ruth*

## Good Morning

Cheep.
Cheep, tweet.
Tweet, cheep, chirp.
Chirp, twitter.
Peep.
Cheep, cheep, twitter, tweet, cheep, chirp.
Wh-coooo, coooo, coooo.
Twitter, trill, peep, chirp, chirp.
Cheep, cheep, cheep, tweep, chirp, twit.
Chirp, twitter, twitter, cheep, cheep, peep,
    chirp, coooo, twip-tweep, coooo,
    peep, cheep, chirp, peep, twitter, twitter,
    cheep, peep.
Twir, tweet.
Twir, twir.
Peep.

## I Hadn't Planned to Love You

I hadn't planned to love you quite as much
but years and joys, hurts and love
beyond anything I could imagine when I was 20
have done it to me.
More than enough.

There is nothing in me that does not love you.
Turn me inside out - there is less of me
than there is love for you.

When we are done,
you and I,
will it be enough?
No.

But for each moment
each everything
the all of you that you have given me
for now
I am
your Ruth.

*50th wedding anniversary*

## Morning Exercise

A gray bird
straddles two outside sprigs
near the top of the Austrian pine in our back yard,
jouncing up and down
with avian grace.
A mini-trampoline dance
for him and me
at breakfast.

## Of Two Minds

I had a mind.
It got me up each morning.
I fixed breakfast
and read the crummy news in the crummy paper.
I paid it no heed.

Then one day it started to leave.
I didn't notice.
I still got up,
fixed breakfast
and read the crummy news in the crummy paper.

My husband noticed,
took me by the ear
and asked the brain doctor,
    "What's wrong?"
The doctor said,
    "I'll take a look."

That doctor said to another doctor,
    "What is this goop?
    It doesn't belong in a brain.
    It will bother her mind.
    We will take this goop out!"
They did.

I now get up in the morning,
fix breakfast,
listen to music,
see the sunrise
and know the joy to have a mind.

## Prescription Question

Are these words
words that sing,
words not to be forgotten?
Or are these words
words made new
by doses of Dilantin?

## Shirley

Such a silly,
    Shirley.
Peppermint ice cream
    dipped in chocolate
    and in a sugar cone, please.
Teen-wise girls when Saturday meant
    the beach
    where we oiled and burned in two-piece abandon.
You said I showed you California clouds
    and firs and golden poppies on a spring blue-lupined hill.
You told me once you never thought about those red roses
    that bloom cascading upwards
    to cover a wall, a fence, or a county.
Or saw patterns the hillside grass turns into
    when wind replaces Bay fog.
Sights and smells, ordinary to you, but new and a
    different beautiful to someone from Iowa.
Funny Shirley.
Loving Shirley.
I wish you were here to laugh and giggle
    and eat too much ice cream with me.

# The Professional

The Thing, lizard-like,
  grows,
    tail flung in expert casualness across the eyes,
loathsome weight heavy.

Body, grotesque as Hell,
    stuffs its swelling self
    into the filling space that was,
becoming Death's slime.

Is this how Hell takes us?
How its master makes us his?
    A little,
    then more,
    and all consumed.
We scarcely notice.

Eons make it easy.
    He does it every day.
He is, in and out of time,
    a Professional.

This time a knife strikes him down.
    We are rescued, saved.
The lizard-shadow races out.

A moment and the
    bloodied, cut-off tail re-grows
    whole, before our unbent eyes.

Another body?
    Easy.
Another mind?
    Of course.
Another soul?
    Just his job.

## The Search

It shot into the sky so fast
I did not know it was the moon.

When I looked I could not look,
its face had turned into a light so bright
my eyes were closed part way.

A seeking incandescence shone upon the earth.
Light so strange it hurt a bush it lingered on,
and the wakened squirrel drew back, dismayed.

A piece of ground, just sleeping,
    too, was roused,
        questioned, before the brightness hurried on.

Pale morning came too soon.
A wearied moon.
An empty search.

Foolish moon, he is not here.
You should have turned your face around
and looked in those great, bright heavens beyond the stars.

A light not half of yours would find him there.

*dedicated to Marion L. Shane*

## While

While the rest of the world is kept busy
trying to set 8:03
and getting 9:06
on those damn digital clocks,
the Japanese have bought Los Angeles.

# [ 1990 ]

### A Parting

The left side and
the right side of my brain
have come to a parting of the way.
Left side says to right,
"Remember!!"
Right side says to left,
"I'd rather play."

## Academic Genealogy

Are you of the House of Strong Vincent?
Descended from the lineage of Academy?
Was East High or Tech your ancestral hall?

The local school genealogists
box you in a moment
asking where you went to high school.

Say you're not from this town
their eyes glaze over.
They are talking to a nobody.

## Yo, Brutus – A Letter to Amy

I'd like to blame it on someone,
my childhood, or being dropped on my head.
The great-grandmother of my grandpa,
a progenitor, long ago dead.

I'd like to blame it on something,
a chromosome, nicked, gone astray.
A flaw in the genes, a blip in the brain,
a fault in the old DNA.

The curse belongs on the time of the month?
A moon phase? Saturn coterminous in Mars?
An electrical field has caused all this grief?
The problem is all in the stars?

(chorus)

> Hyperploid,
> Sigmund Freud
> Yo, Brutus,
> Who's to say.

The day was just about perfect,
the soft court bliss on our feet.
We glided, we leaped, we ran after shots.
Our joy with the tennis complete.

Really, I'm sorry, Amy.
And feel plain stupid , too.
I wouldn't do anything
to hurt such a dear friend as you.

In searching about for a reason
only one thought comes to me.
My behavior descends from an ancestor
who hung by his tail from a tree.

> Exeunt,
> Ruth

## Worry Train

There's a worry train that leaves here
about a quarter after four.
It makes stops at six and seven
so you can pile on more and more
of ordinary worries.
Worries you're quite fond of.
Worries you abhor.

Worries saved from yesterday.
Worries all brand new.
Worries since you're forty.
Worries learned at two.

Worries that are frightening.
Worries that are fun
to talk about and play with
until you understand
that you're the Man
with worries.

Worry ... worry ... worry Train.
In the distance sounds so fine.
Those are other peoples' worries there.
Closer? They are mine.

# [ 1992 ]

## Joy

Joy rushed out to meet me,
arms outstretched
and drew me close.
It was like it never left.
I know it all again, so well,
yet, too long since it was here.

# [ 1994 ]

## February Morning on Peach Street

In prōcess slow we meet,
two columns funereal lit,
lights not to see but seen.
Each one passes us,
cars filled with no one
showing nothing where someone was.

A whitened hill, gained
with careful foot, gloved hands.

An only sound the intermittent blade
that pushes off vague snow,
but does not clear shroud of fog
nor banish slick.

Lights on, we, they, come,
singly,
and disappear in the morning.

## Your Song

I tried to play your song this morning.

In my head
        it plays and plays
        sings and moves
        the rhythms are right
        and the music won't stop,
        the sounds
        the tones
        the chords
        the melody.
It's all there and won't let me think of anything else.

Try them on the piano
they are not on any keys,
but between sharps and flats,
some by half
some by a third or less.

Do you have other notes I can hear?
Or must I take up the violin?

# [ 1995 ]

### A Saint in Training

*We do what we can and*
  *we pray for what we cannot yet do.*
    St. Augustine


An untidy place, this Catholic church
where babies cry at Mass
and the priest says "us"
when he talks about who isn't perfect.
I heard the place was for sinners,
so I just showed up.

## Sunday Mass

Babies wail.
Backs ache from hard chairs.
Knees hurt from wooden kneelers.
We stand throughout the Offertory.

A boy of two or three
gets away from a row of parents
and wanders up to the altar,
to the Presence.

Our priest blows his nose on a huge handkerchief
which he stuffs into a side pocket
just underneath the ritual cassock.
Somehow he is not lessened in his office
as server of the Sacrifice.

A messy group,
these Catholics,
shuffling through the Divine Offering,
Salvation Mystery,
Holiest of Holies come to be with and within us,
God Incarnate.

# [ 1996 ]

*hurry*

*hurry*
*hurry*
*not enough time*
*don't relax*
*don't think ahead*
*too*
*so*
*very*
*scary*
*many*
*things to do*
*before I'm*
*dead.*

## I'm Glad I Kissed Each Flower

I'm glad I kissed each flower,
held each one to my breast.
I'm glad I loved each hour,
made every day the best.
Felt every feeling,
thought every thought,
savored each loving,
owned all my oughts.
I'm glad I had each moment,
hurt and joy, pain, caress.
Frightened oh so often,
grateful for God's yes.

## Late Spring Comes to the Peninsula

Surreptitiously,
like miscreant, mischievous children
near unknowing, unseeing, unaware elders,
they have coated themselves in growing green velour.
A miniature fairy forest world emerges,
bush-bursting with spring beginnings,
shouting alive in a verdant key, unheard.

Far above in a too-late-cold May sky
bony-fingered branches rub up against the gray
in futile pokes
seeking a season that should be here.

Thick, brown-solid trunks
plunged straight deep in frigid sandy soil
know nothing.
Wait for something forgotten.
Longed for
with the ache of not having.

## Marriage Encounter - Encountered Too Often

I'm tired this morning.
My eyes are like glue.
Somebody phoned us
last night – was it you?
There we were sleeping
snug in our bed
when suddenly happened
that sound that we dread,
the telephone ringing,
ring-ey one, two or three.
Is it Marriage Encounter?
Or a real caller for me?

We truly enjoyed
our time in November.
A worthwhile encounter
for us to remember.
A valuable tool
making things clear.
Writing our feelings
to the one we hold dear.
But now that we're home,
can you guess what will happen?
There's one, ring-ey two
whenever we're nappin'.

We're home for the day.
The dishes are done.
Evening has settled.
It's time for some fun.
For us that means TV,
a movie or so.
A time to relax,
unwind and let go.
A time to share stories.
How's Ruth and how's Joe.
Ring-ey one; Ring-ey two.
Pu-leeeze – No, no and no.

Picture us settled,
snoozed in our chair.
The telephone rings.
There's nobody there.
We're in the basement.
We tear up the stair.
Wrong number?
It's beginning to wear.
We know you mean well,
but, please, if you care,
no more fun phone calls.
that's our prayer.

## Not From the Portuguese Sonnets

How dost thee not love me?
Thou hast no feeling?

Thou sayest love
when I do thee good.
Yet I feelest none
where there shouldst
be much or some.

But nothing.
Naught,
where ought
to be
Some feeling.

Canst thou not speak it?
I think thee can
but feelest not.

Thy limbic
and thy verbal neocortex
seldom speak
to each other.

I wish they could
for I wouldst hear these words.

## The Pig Iron Press

The Pig Iron Press has come to town
to read your poems upside down.
Doesn't know and doesn't care
who or what or why's in there.
Bring fifteen copies, more or less.
What you've written we'll mess
up and say you're making progress.

Thank you, no, that one's done.
I'm working on another one.
I won't be there, Pig Iron Press.
Thanks the same or more or less.

Who's Whose Self

What's in there
that won't be let out
won't be found?

Won't.
Can't.
Don't.
Will not.

Will not see or feel or touch.
Busy instead of.

Walk around.
Pretend.
No, not pretend.

Push down.
Ignore.
Avert
so you won't see.
A self.
A you.

Too much there?
Or too little?

[ 1997 ]

A Definition of God

God
is
both the question
and
the
answer.

Why?
Why.

## Anna Freundel

She sits in one of the four chairs,
beige-gray waiting room chairs.
After 77 years
here she is today.

Thinned away.
Glasses, permed hair.
Sweet face, big nose.
An accent that still says eu in u.

1952 brought her to Amerika with her husband.
Dead now these five years.
Cancer, too.
There were no children.

Her four friends, couples,
now are gone.
Wearing green gowns
we talk.

Waiting,
for X-rays to reveal
what's inside
besides loneliness.

## April Snow

Bow down little daffodils,
So brave
So dancing
With Spring's merriment.

Foolish little flowers
Dared try to be
Dared try to be pretty
Tried to do your daffodil thing.

Haven't you heard?
Don't you know?
Life is hard
Joy and beauty fleeting.

Please come back.
We need you
For it to be
April.

## February 9

Ten minutes to wait.
I stop the car near bushes
facing old, dim houses
across the street.

Snow in single separate flakes
falls from a sky not much higher than the tree tops.
Each descends gently, inevitably down
       from close, gray beginnings,
its brief life encompassed between the near sky
and a hard not-cold street
       where it quietly melts into no more.

It had no chance
       to be a part of a snowman,
       played in by wet children,
       shoveled by weary grownups at the end of a day,
       or scraped noisily
       into a soon to be dirt-darkened pile at streetside
       by unfeeling blades of a plow.

It doesn't stay outside, that snow,
but comes into my car,
flakes into and on my soul.

It's time to leave.
Just soon enough
before I, too, am consumed in this melting.

## Invisible

You can't see me,
I'm invisible.

This face you see?
Fooled you!
Isn't me.

I'm in here.

Sometimes I laugh.
Sometimes I play peek-a-boo,
but you don't know.

Go ahead,
look at me.

Think you've found me?
Nope.
Not today.

I'm way, way, way
way in here.

By myself.

## PET Scan

They took a PET scan of his brain
and found a huge mass
that occupied most of his head,
a mass that pulsed
and throbbed.

They X-rayed it,
took a biopsy
and finally,
brought in the doctor,
a small man with glasses
and a yellow pencil behind his ear.

"Ah, yes," he said, glancing at the tests,
"I do recognize the reddish brown color.
That's a mass of Hate.
See it move?
It eats itself
and therefore grows
until it fills the brain."

"What can we do for him?" we cried.
"I don't know," he sighed.
"There's a little tiny, shriveled white lump here.
See?
That's a remnant of Love.
And see that small pale blue area?
That's Caring.
But it may be too late."

# Roots

"What?
Move again?
No, I don't believe it!
It's happened so often over the years
and, finally,
finally,
I've put down roots,
made friends,
bought some curtains that match the couch.
I don't believe it!
It's going to be very hard to leave after all this time."

I looked down,
felt beneath my feet,
moved one big toe,
and saw those roots.
There they were.
Thirty years of them.
A quarter of an inch deep.

## Waiting for Laura

Five-year-old Laura arrives.
She is here to make orange rolls.
We are ready and the dough is in the bowl,
waiting.

But after hugs and kisses
she doesn't come into the kitchen.
She sits down at the top of the stairs,
takes a pencil and a pink-and-purple tablet
from her little-girl purse and begins to write,
slowly making letters into words.

She prints, erases, makes a mark,
erases once more,
gripping her pencil tightly.
The point breaks off.
She runs to sharpen it and writes again.
Not quite right, erased.

At last, silence.
Laura places her pencil and tablet into her purse,
zipping it tightly.
Then, racing up the stairs she stands beaming before us
and holds out a rumpled paper with two lines of careful printing,
words that read,

"I love you, Grandma.
I love you, Grandpa."

# [ 1999 ]

## Monday Visitors

They arrive at the door,
two men in black pants and white shirts,
narrow black ties.
Earnest and polite.

Small,
sincere but eager.

Each wears glasses with thin frames.
Very now.

They want to save my soul
and won't take much of my time.

It's a good thing that
half of my hair is up in rollers,
and the other half
can't wait for my soul to be saved.

I'm too busy
this Monday morning.

## My Mother and I

If you were 5 and I was 5,
    would we play dolls together?
    Have tea and be veddy grown up
    with pudgy pinkies extended just so?
Would we be friends?

If you were 10 and I was 10,
    would there be sleepovers
    where we giggled and laughed
    and tried to stay up late
    eating popcorn,
calling out, "We're almost asleep."

If you were 15 and I was 15,
    would we hang out together,
    phone when we were apart
    and talk over our life that day,
complaining, "Nobody else understands."

At 20? At 50?
Would we be friends?
Could we be friends?

No.
I was never 5
and you were never 15.

## October

What happened?
When October came all modesty, all decorum left.
You went from sturdy, solid, mature and serene. Quiet.
Overnight you changed.
You began to move, to feel with the wind first pale touches of yellow.
A tinge. Then a pink. An orange.
Next a whole limb thrust out a bronze and a gold.
Then half of you burst into crimson.

Your companions were just as bad.
Rust-colored rowdies, all of you turned raucous shades of reds
    in hues and shades and tints more than there are names.
You became a moving flirt, a wanton, a frolic.
A romp, a game, a bawdy display of outrageous beauty.
Immodest, inflamed, tossing about in a teasing air.
Fiery in desire burning yourself.
You all were naughty show-offs, outdoing each other
    in noisy shouting colors.

Your movements, swept by a breeze, became more bold.
You caught the eye of any who tried to look past you.
Brazen in dress, in attitude, you multi-colored hoyden.
Smoldering in bright afternoons against backdrops of blue.
Until at last you cast yourself into an ecstasy of brilliance
    which you cannot stop.

All shame is shed to these tenth-month winds.
Baring yourself in sudden surges of flying.
Undressing yourself on any hapless green lawn.
Pretending those jewels are worth it.
You throw yourself into the arms of any willful breeze that tugs at you
    and you are totally naked. Shameful.

November.
You are thin.
Bare-boned.
Limbs revealed as black.
Spare.
Austere.
Now you say you are sorry.
You repent.
You almost cannot remember what for.

How can you make us think that flaunting lusty scarlet was not you?
Yesterday's intensity is forgotten.
So.
Now you are pure?
Sterile, even.
Grace is begged from unloving skies with chastened, outstretched fingers.

Try to pretend you are holy.
I know you.
When May comes
You'll be saucy.
You'll dance in beginning green, flirting with us all again.
Covered in blossoms.

The coquette.

## View From My Window

A dime-size tan spider
    waits on the screen
        above the sink

            - for me to leave?

Wasting shapes of last week's snow
    diminish themselves
        on bleak grass.

Three always-green blue spruce
    rest patiently,
        tops full of dangled cones.

A twiggy red bush takes itself up high in thin lines
    above bare ground,
        warming its life.

In the far yard
    sits a cold white birch
        too elegant to share with seasons.

Beyond tall penciled trees
    rests a blue sky
        gray washed
            with thinned out,
                leaving,
                    almost-once clouds.

A twisted glass icicle
    drips quietly
        in the March morning.

# [ 2000 ]

### Bonnie's Car

The leather-laced wheel
    feels just right to the touch.
An expanse of dash and dials
    is trimmed with real walnut.

The multi-informational display
    with clock, compass, calendar and outside temperature
    tells you when and weather where you are.
Montana leather, heated, lumbar supported,
    10-way adjustable memory-encoded seats
    keep you constant in your comfort.

In winter, snow slides from warmed outside mirrors,
    while traction control and ABS keep you safe,
    and rain-sensing wipers keep you seeing.

In summer, the power, two-way sliding moon-roof
    opens to bring God's stars in for your private viewing,
    and a filtration system allows no pollen or dust
    to enter your cabin,
        your home.

You and your passenger can enjoy
    individual temperatures from the
    dual automatic climate control
as you listen to the soul of
    Beethoven, 'N Sync or Debussy
    from your 200-watt, 10-speaker anti-theft audio system.

And if you have no passenger,
    no one to share this ride with you,
take your safety-caged structure,
    with side and front air bags,
    head restraints and anti-lock 4-wheel disc brakes,
and use that 210 hp 2.5 inline 6 to get where you're going.

Let satellite navigation see, if it can,
    that your thinned-out, exercised body,
    your face, still lovelier than a Juliet,
cover a self already in a thousand pieces.

On a clear autumn Saturday afternoon
    around two,
at a crossing south of town, she drove her new silver luxury car
    around the gate and waited for the train.

## Losers

I wouldn't play Scrabble with her.
She always had to win,
    chortled when she did.
We didn't play
        and both lost.

## Lunch at the Club

We sat 'neath the gable
at our country club table
Vi, Helen and Mabel
      and me,
dainty white skirts to the knee.

We had come from the court,
tennis our sport,
decorum our forte,
      e.g.,
no ball hit in anger you'd see.

In our regular places
with healthy, bright faces
watching sailboating races
      for free,
sipping orange juice and coffee and tea.

Our morning meal wishes
are served on Club dishes;
we're always called "Mrs."
      by Bea.
We visit and gaze out to sea.

There are white caps that curve,
blue skies to observe –
"Would you care for preserve?
      More tea?
Marmalade, butter or brie?"

"Girls, the game was well played!"
"Vi, the backhands you made!!"
"Mabel, your shots ricocheted
      by me!"
"The score was 6-2 and 6-3!!"

"The serves were plain vicious!"
"Helen's half-volleys delicious."
"Bea, this toast's most nutritious."
      Ah, me.
Four lovely ladies are we.

We nattered, we chattered
of things that then mattered.
Reputations were shattered
      with glee
by Mabel, Vi, Helen and me.

Then talk turned to Texas.
Crime was the nexus.
And they, as they breakfast,
      agree
on ending a man such as he.

"I think he should die,"
murmur Helen and Mabel and Vi.
"That Texan should fry."
      "Yes, he
sounds plenty guilty to me."

Vi buttered her muffin,
"Yes, Gary's a tough one,
a mean and a rough one,"
      says she.
"Toast 'em and roast 'em, i.e."

"He's had a raw deal."
"There's been an appeal."
"His guilt is for real."
    "No plea.
In Texas he doesn't go free."

"His son's in jail too."
"And what did he do?"
There was something to rue,
    you see,
crime runs in the family tree.

"Oh, fie, let him die."
"I say hang him high."
"Anyone for more pie?"
    Friends three.
Lunch here is served with ennui.

## Summer Vacation As Remembered by Joe

Every summer we went to the country, the farm.
    ...all right, the farm was two acres.

The wide expanse of green lasted the whole summer.
    ...so, it was a month.

There were many animals for us city boys to see.
    ...well, two chickens and a pig.

At the end of the land there was a rushing stream.
    ...o.k., only after a heavy rainstorm.

A very big, deep swimming hole kept us cool.
    ...dissolved sulfur from the mines turned our skin orange.

I developed my aquatic skills there.
    ...my uncle threw me in so I had to learn fast.

I became a skilled and wise gambler there.
    ...we played poker for penny matches.

We had an alfresco place for dining.
    ...I hung my feet out the barn loft to eat ice cream.

There is where my boxing career began and ended.
    ...tennis seemed a safer sport.

I ran.   I played.   I ran.   I played.
    ...I never stopped.

## The Best Love

The best love
    doesn't come with crashing explodes of fireworks
    shooting through a star-and-moon filled sky,
    bursts of color-crescendos,
    tumult and light filling my universe.

But, when I
    reach out toward you across the bed
    and feel your warmth before I touch you
        a softened rain falling outside under a quiet wet sky,
        thunder and lightning far away
        barely heard, scarcely seen,

then love comes
    and all the earth shifts slowly in its molten center
    reaching and embracing us,
    making us one
        again.

## Young Davids

Young Davids,
    dressed in dark jackets,
    white shoes that don't quite touch the ground.
Suspended in time and place.

Young Davids,
    not held anywhere
    by sculpted stone.
Night brings them out.

Last year
    or the year before
    they were shouting, stick-wielding boys
playing street hockey on roller blades.

Now a half dozen or more
    briefly stop our car,
    not-linked arms wave us through.
Smiling, they ask us for a ride.

Young Davids,
    unknowing of their beauty,
    their promise just beginning.
Their time to become.

Angels, be with them.
    Hover over them.
    Keep them safe.
Young Davids on our street.

# [ 2001 ]

### Attendance at Mass

Though
attendance is
required,
obligation became
want
need
desire
food
drink
life
breath
a long time ago.

# E-mail

I sent an e-mail to You,
    God,
several of them.

Instant communication
    Right?
    I wonder.
Was the POP down?

Several days later,
    an answer.
Not what I expected
    but o.k.

Not sure who
Your server
    Is.

## Logos

Was the first Logos just a whisper?
What was that Word,
the Word uttered?

Was it done in Joy?
Loneliness?
An atom seized by error?

All those learned people
say they are certain
how it all began.

I don't know.
I just see
He sure started something.

Here we are,
you and me,
the Plan.

## Nonny

Going
from
our
love
to God's
love
and
all those waiting there.

It is so hard
to let her go
even to You.

## Sunday Morning Daughters

Outside in early morning
they take the air,
pushed about in their carriages.
Dressed in good clothes.
Lined faces, heads in bent resignation.

Do they know that their daughters,
grandmothers themselves,
are not at Sunday Mass
so they can take mother
outdoors on God's Day?

## The 22nd Day of Snow

Like torn pieces of Kleenex
the sky descends on my day.

There must be a lot of crying
for something or someone
here or there.

Whether sadness or joy
a white beauty falls,
cold and briefly lovely.

Pain or happiness.
One of us cannot tell the difference.

## The Universe Up Close

The small
dark
paneled room
was lit by a single shaft of sunlight
where
shining golden bits of dust
rode up and down
on unseen strings,
balanced
as carefully
as the universe
holds
its weighted stars.

## The Wind Blows Where It Will
*John 3:8*

One day it touched me,
third person of the Trinity,
Spirit itself fit into Ruth size.
All that is life
light
song
infinite power,
in gentleness and joy.

Some day
in a way I cannot imagine,
it will come again.

## When You Grow Old
*John 21:18*

...when you grow old
they will bathe you on
Thursdays and Mondays at 8,
speak to you in voices
that are too loud,
bring pills of many colors,
purgatives and salves
to help you.

They will remind you,
the friends you talk to
are not always there,
and it is time now
to take your nap.

When you grow old,
when I grow old,
be close, my God,
keep me in your arms.
Let me not lose sight also
of Thee.

# [ 2002 ]

## Cry

I cry
not because you are not here now.
I cry for all the things
that never happened
the words never said
the love never shown
the look never given
the touch never felt
the smile not seen.

And can't now.

## Gherkins

Gherkins can lurk in a
bottle of brine
fat little cucumbers
all of them mine.

# Home

Well.
Finally, I'm here.
It took long enough.

Those two weeks on a table in the living room,
then that long ride,
    bouncing along
    with everyone talking.

We turned at last where a quiet grove of pines
    presses solidly into blue Lassen County sky.
    And sunshine through sturdy trunks lies in spots
    on light brown ground.

Away from the real road
    into a space between the trees that is a sort of road,
    on to stone-edged flat clearings,
    to you, my love.
And our son, who hasn't been here very long.

They were very gentle,
    those three 40-something grandchildren, Mary,
    and Paul, our last.
I liked what RuthAnn said,
    and how Jim and Joe
    edged aside enough of the cool earth for me.

Dust to dust, as they say.

They snugged me down,
    patting the surface smooth again.
Talked a while
    and then they left
    late in the afternoon.

I'm back.
    Where I wanted to be.
    Where I belong.

White pines whisper to each other
    into mountain air that is only air,
    into blue and blue of skies that are only here.

It is peace. It is quiet.

I don't know if this is heaven, but I'm home.

## It's Not Just Getting There

We used to talk about Heaven,
she and I,
now and then.

She knew she was going there,
never if,
only when.

She knew who would be there,
her aunts and
her mother,

two husbands, her grandma,
two sisters,
one brother.

Friends from her lifetime,
just seven.
She named them.

Her church folk, politicians,
the famous.
She claimed them.

In Heaven would be Jesus,
arms outstretched
open wide,

his loving compassion
bringing her close
to his side.

She died as she planned,
arriving in Heaven
that night.

As she had expected,
it was a
beautiful sight.

But the first soul she saw
gave her quivers
and shakes.

Her mean, nasty, old Dad!
Does Heaven
make mistakes?

She yelled at St. Peter,
"Is this some kind
of joke?

You've got to be kidding!
Heaven's meant for us
good folk!"

Whispered one pearly angel,
holding on to
his hat,

"That's not how we work here.
It's 'sinners saved' and
all that.

You got here by grace
and we have a pretty
fine view.

If you want to go elsewhere
that's all up
to you."

## Requiescat Bells

In the name of the Father
    *claraclaraclaraclara*
The Son
    *eberpaulinearthur*
The Holy Spirit. Amen
    *clyde*
Almighty and merciful God
    *John...John...John*
Cherish the souls Thou hast created
    *billie billie billie billie*
In the hour of their going forth
    *shirley shirley shirley*
Presented without stain of sin to Thee
    *paul paul paul paul*
By the hands of the holy angels
    *sarah sarah*
The adversary may not prevail
    *frank frank frank frank*
In thee, O Lord, have I hoped
    *david david*
Come upon these gifts
    *annette annette annette*
The Body
    *joseph*
The Blood
    *ruth*

Requiem aeternam dona eis, Domine:
et lux perpetua lucent eis.

Author's note: Each line of names or one name is a bell that rings with its own tone and rhythm.

## Requiescat in Pacem

In the name of the Father, the Son and the Holy Spirit. Amen.

*Eber, Pauline, David, Shirley, Norma, John, Billie*

Almighty and merciful God, cherish the souls Thou has created in the hour of their going forth.

*Sarah, Paul, Jennie, Nana, Frank, Nonny, Pete, PJ*

Presented without stain of sin to Thee by the hands of the holy angels

*Sonny, Terry, Dorothy, Buck, Helen, Ruthcarroll*

The adversary may not prevail. In Thee, O Lord, have I hoped.

*Dale, Dorothy H., Grace, Joseph, Ruth*

Come upon these gifts. The Body, the Blood.

Requiem aeternam dona eis, Domine: et lux perpetua lucent eis.

## Supply Work

When I knelt in that darkened confessional,
haltingly telling you of measly sins
done since last I saw you,
I felt I was truly touching the finger of God,
woman in Michelangelo's *Creation*.

When I took part in
or observed
or merely was there
for weekly Mass,
the Consecration was the Body and the Blood,
and you our priest enabled to be priest
for us the ordinary folk.

Now our Bishop, The Most Reverend,
tells us you were there doing supply work,
a.k.a.
saying Mass
hearing confessions.

Our fine,
old,
reassigned,
pedophile
priest.

## The Attack

All day long you pummel me
hammer at me.
I cannot think.

You a's
and h's and l's.
Those c's and e's and j's.
The o's.

Night, too.
You do not leave me alone,
d's, and s's,
q's and y's.

All the rest,
surely more than 26.

Jumbled
and pushed
and jammed and smashed,
crammed.

So loud.

Into words
that sing
shout
laugh
and hurt.

Words that won't let me be.

## The Women Next Door

She had a lump on her neck.
So did her mother.
They lived there.
They died there
one after the other.

# [ 2003 ]

### The Obit Page

Faces look out from the page
or pages,
depending.

Young, she smiles from a day perhaps 40 years ago
when her hair was long and brown,
combed back from a smooth forehead.

Another sees sturdily straight ahead,
eyes, even with glasses,
observing everything.

An older man, gray and white hair,
has his mouth partly open
as if in mid sentence.

Some serious, but most with the smiles of living,
Fixed in a day, there,
before they went on to the next moment.

# [ 2004 ]

### A Blanket of Birdsong

When I wakened this morning
a blanket of birdsong covered me.

Solid, heavy and dense,
it lay thick between me and God's sky,
a soft layer of un-seamed, downy music
greeting the new day.

I did not notice
when,
note by note,
feather, trill and chirp,
it slowly thinned,
dissolving into separate voices.

Birds, singing by twos or threes,
or singly into an ordinary blue sky.

## A Pickle

Here lies a pickle
soaking in juice,
sighing and crying,
"Boohoo, what's the use?"

A dill's just a frill
to embellish a relish,
green on your plate,
cucumbered fate.

Slice it or dice it,
shades of chartreuse.
Sad little pickle,
a veggie excuse.

## Anxious Annie

Why so anxious, Annie?
Why worry, fret and stew?
Will they hate you
if you're late again?
Does it matter if they do?

Why hurry, hurry, hurry?
You only bother you.

# Celebration in the Barnyard

*as written by
an Albuquerque Barred Plymouth Rock hen
and one rooster*


Here's cluckcluckcluckcluck pluuuck
Come, cluck!

Oh, chickchickchick chiiiick
Come, quick!

Come cheer...cheer...cheer cheeeer...
Come, here!

Cock, comerevelrevelrevel too
Cockcock, hooray!

Cel ebraaatebraaaatebrate braaaate
Ole'!

I diiidiiiiddiiiiddiddid diiid it
Today!

Gaather......
gaather.......
gaather.......

See??
An egg!!!!

## Little Gus

"Help me, help me,"
gasped good little Gus.
"I'm barely into your nose.
I'm trying to get
from this place on your face
    to your elbows,
    your knees
    and your toes.
I'm just a breath of fresh air.
Oh, please –
    God Bless me,
    a sneeze!"

## My Friends

A long time ago I looked for a pool,
at a health club, a Y or even a school,
to lose some of my flab and hanging down skin,
to work into shape, try to get thin.

"Villa's the place," a friend told me one day,
"you'll do water aerobics, have fun, even play."
I ran to the attic for suit, goggles and hat.
But where was I going? Where was it at?
Lo! There was a sign about Ms. Audrey E. Sweny,
her dollars and dimes had built a pool for us many.

I zipped to the lockers, showered and suited,
walked to the pool, where voices grew muted.
A sylph with a smile said, "Hello, come right in.
We're so glad you're here, now let us begin.
This is Dorothy and Sue, Shirley, Millie and Liz,
and there's my aunt, Margaret Anne, a real lolly-wiz."
Six friendly ladies, a nice little bunch.
When class time was over they asked me to lunch.

I came back the next week, the next month and more.
Our hips grew more limber, our backs not as sore.
We exercised every thing, muscles galore,
moving and swishing to a musical score.
We did polkas and Cocuzzi from our own Pennsylvania,
Glen Miller, chicken dances and learned the Macarena.
We splashed and we stretched, dug holes in the water.
"Peggy," we shivered, "this pool's gotta be hotter."

Now, we splash, stretch, circle, bend, swivel and flex
our knees, feet and hips, our lips and our necks.
Our chassis are looser, our fingers, our toes,
elbows and shoulders, ears, chins, knees and nose.
We move and we twist, feet point wide and then narrow.

We march, knees held high. We step over that barrel.
We say "Yes" to "Are your tummies held tight?"
(We're under water, so we're outa sight.)
We rise on our toes for all-over squeezes, then
stop what we're doing to count Millie's sneezes.

We talk and we sing, we dance and we yak,
we walk fro and to, and then we walk back.
We giggle, we wiggle, we laugh very loudly.
Our posture is perfect, our chests held out proudly.
We try frog/scissor kicks (done very badly).
Most times we're happy, some times we're sadly.
By the end of the hour we're soggy but glad,
with pool exercise over, there's lunch to be had.

We've known many friends as time has gone by,
new friends became old friends and some said goodbye.
Ginny and Dorothy, Fifi, Millie and Fran,
Marilu and Mary Lou, Lois, Grace, Terry and Jan,
Adeline, Marian, Marie, two Mary Anns,
Audrey, Vienna, Barb, both of the Shirleys,
Carol and Claire, Chris, Liz, all of you girlies,
Judie, Dolores, Pat S., Sandy, and Lea,
Nelda, Val, Peggy, you're all special to me.

Ends have beginnings; beginnings have ends.
I wish we could stay in the middle,
but it's time for goodbyes to my friends.

        with love and thanks to all of you
            from your friend,
                Ruth

## The Peacock

The Indian prince steps carefully from his high branch
    down to a tree stump,
    thin legs landing him awkwardly on dusty ground below.
He lifts his Marine-cut crested head, surveying,
    then steps forward with deliberate solemnity,
    glistening green and cobalt neck
    gently thrusting him forward in a late spring afternoon.
An iridescent train of feathers drag behind, holding him back.

    But,
    wait!
    he senses...
    yes, a maiden!!
    nearby, but where?
    No matter,
    he seeks!

Slowly, he unfolds the rapturous display that is his glory,
    a fan of jeweled blues and greens and browns.
Eyed-ornaments
    that rajahs envied and Solomon and Pharaohs desired.
    He turns,
    reverses himself,
    circles again,
    moves backward in ungainly dance,
    then forward once more.
The dandy. The glorious dandy.

But where is the object of his desire?
No lady appears.
Only a gray and white Rhode Island hen,
    slightly plump in her feathers.
Was it she? She who so aroused?
This fluff has foolishly confused his maleness?

Plumage sagging he retreats, remounts the stump
    and flaps his labored way to the top of a shed,
    where he cries out his peacock call,
    loud and louder.

# [ 2005 ]

### Delfino

Did they....
        have you wear a helmet?
        tell you to be careful?
        brace that pile of dirt that fell onto you?
        walk over to see how you were doing?
            *no minuto?*
                <u>no</u> time
        *muy occupado?*
                very, <u>very</u> busy
        *muy remoto?*
                40 feet is far away

Did they....
        tell OSHA?
            *mañana, Si*
        have safety,
            *explicar en Español?*

No need if nothing ever
        *occurir*
        that could cost
        *mucho dinero*
        *mas mas dolares*

Each of these, as they say,
        regrettable oversights,
        could have cost el Texas company
            $7000,
                *siete mil*

Your worth, coste, Delfino, for an afternoon
*totalizar $28,750*

39 years old,
*Delfino Martinez, 39 años.*

## His Passion

I did not know the passion
he felt for me when he was 26
the hurts he would risk
    to have me.

An inner self so intense
    I did not see it.

We had two children
    he worked
    came home.

He loved me quietly and always
    I did not know him
    as he knew me.

Does love blind?
    Or reveal?

With years together we are old,
    I see now that passion
    which was always there.

## Litany for Philip

Blessed be the donor, strong.
Blessed be his stem cells, given.
Blessed are those who become
    Asclepius/Aesculapius, healers.

Blessed be food, eaten.
Blessed be laughter, shared.
Blessed be true friends, touched.
Blessed be wife, yours.

Blessed be love, said.
Blessed be life, returned.

## Prayer Place

My prayer place
    is a weathered wooden bench
    half way down the dock that extends into marshlands.
An ancient place where fisher-folk prayed by this river.
I have come to seek your same Great Spirit.

Today, far away in all the green and wetness
    stands one still, white egret.
The diurnal undeniable force of an incoming tide
    streams faster than I'd think it could.

Far enough away a lone fisherman
    checks his four crab buckets,
    nods hello,
    and returns to his own space at the end of the dock.

Hear me...Spirit
    Keep, I pray, our Margret, from harm.
    Let her be well, stay strong.
    May this dark week be but seven days.

Holy Spirit.
    Here.
    In this prayer place of 10,000 years.

## Rehearsals

What will happen when I die
if I don't know anybody there.

Rehearsed speeches
      for absolution
      forgiveness
      explanations of why,
all for naught...

Unless I give them to people
      I don't know.

Maybe that's how it goes.

## Seasons Greetings

December mailings have brought the cards,
    greetings for the season.

Three Magi ride on camels under a single star.
Large ornaments, green, blue, red, hang on a silver string
    that begins and ends beyond the edge.
A transfixed angel holds its angel chest in unutterable emotion.

Snow cradles a grove of bare birches.
A watercolor Joseph and Mary wade through a brook.
Rust and black-white birds flutter or sit watching
    on a blue-green hat atop a carrot-nosed snowman.

Two poinsettia blooms blaze red.
A white scalloped cathedral gleams.
Stockings, lace trimmed, hang ready.
Fireplace, candles and Christmas tree lights
    glimmer out a window onto sequined snow.

Mary and Joseph marvel at their babe.
A cardinal sits in a beribboned wreath.
Skaters skate a winter pond.
A 17th century village explodes with happy, singing families
    clad in bright woolens.

Mary prays.
Carolers sing in a glittery snow filled yard.
One very large candy cane entices.
Staid gold script wishes Happy Holidays.

Our festive table lies in the late December sun,
    filled with notes and news from loved ones,
    surrounded by memories of those
    who used to send Seasons Greetings.

## What Color Is God

When what is me passes through
tunnel
mist
light
into after and before.
Not trailing eternity,
in it.
Seen finally face to face
all veiling undone.
Brilliance of luminosity.

Will my seeing see?
Will my knowing know?
Sound be sounded?
or
is Joy soundless?
sightless?
unknowing?
lightless?
fullness empty?

Mine
Thine
Is color full.

# [ 2006 ]

## A Poem Is

A poem
is
what's
left
after
everything
else
has been
taken
away.

## Be Careful

Poke a hole,
anywhere.

It will spout
from my elbow
my knee
my arm
my fingers.

Speak to me,
anywhere.

But be careful.
If you nick
even a little bit with your words,
especially those kind ones,
all is liquid.

Skin holds in the tears
that are me.

## Clay Piece
*Isaiah 64:8*

Here I am, Potter,
plopped up, dripping,
off-center.
A blop.

No slab or coil pot for me, please.
I am meant to be a vaaze
thrown slim, perfectly curved,
dried and bisque fired.

Incised, decorated, painted, glazed, then
kiln fired to bring out elegance
beyond imagining.
Perfection.

Here we go, I'm ready!
We're starting, hang on!
Faster, faster! Whoa...ee!
Help!

Where are those promised hands
holding onto my slipperyness?
I'm losing it....
uh ... uh....no.. Oh, no.

This is going to be ugly...
Major splat coming!!
Waaaalls..Flooooor.....
All right. O.k. Get it together.

Ball up and wedge again.
Climb back up again.
Dripping. Centered?
Who knows.

Blop here.
Ready, Potter.

## Genealogy 101

No wonder I'm conflicted,
confused,
don't know what to think.
I'm a mixed-up mess
of DNA.
A potpourri,
an olio,
a stew.

I'm Inuit and Cree.
Sunni and Celt,
Mongol, Maya and Maori,
a DAR whose pedigree dates from Africa.

I'm blood of royals and rascals,
perverts and peculiars,
webs of ordinary folk who lived and died,
for me to be me,
for you to be you.

# I Did Not Believe
*Luke 11:13*

I did not believe.
Yet wanted to believe.
Believe those words
in Genesis, Psalms, Luke and John.
Believe the Spirit is today and was,
not just old stories that we read.
And so I prayed.
Two sentences, I think.
And then went home.

How can I say I saw you, Spirit?
You set a small tree on fire with light.
Alive, it was all of life.

How do I say I heard you, Spirit?
You told me,
"Come and worship.
Come and worship.
Come and worship Christ the King."

How do I say I felt you, Spirit?
Unrelenting joy overcame me.

How do I say anything?
All I have is words.

## Mr. and Mrs. Bentover

Their real name was Jones,
but with bent over bones
everyone called them
the Bentovers.

They bent over to walk,
work, play or talk.
Cooking their suppers, their lowers
were not under their uppers.

If they watched their teevee,
they sat on their settee.
Two little old commas
in matching flowered pajamas.

They used to be upright, head down to toe.
Postures quite perfect a long time ago.
But spines have gone saggy, soggy and beat.
Now their heads are in front of their feet.

Spoon-shaped and aging,
aching and bent,
all of their up-straight
has up and went.

## No Empty Attics

Day by day they come,
trailed by vans from Maine, Ohio.
People, ordinary people,
bringing rose bushes from up north.
A new beginning in this Carolina land of sunshine.

Mostly of an age.
Some alone. Others, couples for one or 60 years.
Road weary they emerge
wearing sandals, shorts, sunglasses,
worn tennis shoes, jeans.

Overnight, high-roofed stucco covered homes
have sprung mushroom-like onto the Lowcountry dirt.
By afternoon sod is in. Palms
and strange southern bushes are growing.
Flag holders in place by garage doors.

The furniture and belongings will fit.
Places will be found for dishes from Aunt Evelyn
and old photographs of unsmiling great-grandparents.
But where to put the memories?
High empty attics are built just for these.

## Patience

Four hundred twenty seven million years ago,
give or take,
in what some day would be called the Silurian period,
a first plant grew out of a little piece of dirt.
No one clapped.
None to shout, "Hooray!"
It just happened.
Very quietly.

Three hundred eighty four million years later,
more or less,
on a special Cretaceous day,
the first plant bloomed.

Does God really have that long?
That much patience?
To wait for one like me?
I think so.
I hope so.
And He will clap
And shout, "Hooray!"

## Praise Song

The sunset
didn't speak Norwegian
the breeze didn't know French
    but since Word first was,
    they sing their song together.

Praise Life!
    Praise Praise!
        Praise All That Is!

## The Word

              That same God
who cracked dark from light,
split the heavens and earth,
skimmed land from sea,
granted time and space dimensions,
flung the galaxies beyond space,
melted stars into the skies,
brought our earth to grow life,
created man,
and then
manifested Himself among us.
The Word
made flesh here for us.
The Christ.

# [ 2007 ]

### Bruce

When
the
earth
turned
back around
here this morning,
one more friend had slid away.
This time it was you, Bruce.

Did you try to hold on?
Grasp that speeding sphere with old fingers?

Nope,
I bet you said,
"Look out!
Here I come!"

# Church

A perfect place to hide...

dim
quiet
dusty
niche filled
empty pews
nervous candles
back-turned droning priest
three bead-fingering women
factory-faced statues cold in worn out colors.

God will never find me here.
I thought.

# Dolly

"You idiot, John, you forgot to put her in the trunk!"

John stopped his big Lexus as fast as he could and slowly stepped out of the car, crunching bits of plastic under his shoes. Part of her head rolled closer to his left foot. Under the wheel, he could see the remainder of a leg, while shreds of the black plastic bag, and splinters and shards of what had been his Louise were everywhere.

"I'm dead," he muttered. "Freedah will blow her top. I can hardly wait." Getting a broom and a dustpan, he swept the garage and the end of the driveway, put all the pieces into a clean trash bag, tied it and went into the house to see his wife.

"Excuse me, Freedah," he interrupted, seeing she was already on the phone, "but when I backed out of the garage I accidentally ran over the mannequin I take on trips. I'm really sorry. Don't worry, I'll get another one when I get to Asheville."

"Hang on, Evie. No, I'll call you back." Freedah glared at John. "Well, if you aren't something! How can a grown man do something so stupid? Sounds just like you, dumb, dumb, dumb, so you should be able to buy another dummy! Lucille...? Wha'd you call her? Louise? Whatever. That store window figurini cost me $35. You better not spend a nickel more! Do you think you can remember? You know what happened in Roanoke."

"Nothing happened in Roanoke, Freedah," snapped John.

"Hah! Well, might have."

"Come on, Freedah. There I was in my motel room after another day on the road. In the middle of the night, that drunk woman comes pounding at the door, rattling the doorknob. What was I supposed to do? I went to see who was there."

"Well, when you went to answer, she'd a come right in if you hadn't had that dummy propped up in the chair facing the door. She thought that blond plastic bimbo was your wife. Hah! Good thing Evie told me to have you buy one of those figurinis. Like she said, it's protection for a lone man, right?"

"Whatever you say. It's time for me to get on the road."

John went back to the car, made sure his sales samples and laptop were in the back seat, and left, driving too fast until he eased onto the main road and then to the highway a few miles away. He began to feel freer as he smoothly edged his way through the heavy traffic and started toward Greenville. He liked to drive.

His day started well. Two probable sales in Greenville, and then back on his way. Another sale in Cashiers, three in Brevard. He always enjoyed the trip up into the North Carolina mountains. Even though highway 64 was full of turns and some 35-mile-an-hour driving, it was relaxing.

He found himself looking over at the empty passenger seat. He would miss the conversations they had had. He was "Jack" and she was Louise, his very blonde girlfriend. He would tell her about his business stops, how well he had done, and all about Freedah. Louise sat there being blonde and plastic, but it was enough.

"Louise," he said to the emptiness, "you and I had some good miles between us. I told you lots of things I never told anybody, and always knew my secrets were safe with you. Finding someone to take your place will be hard. I have to, though, but it won't be another blonde."

Radio reception was nil in the mountains and the trip seemed long because there was no one to talk with. Finally, through the mountains and down, he saw the Asheville city limit sign. Starting to turn toward his usual room at the Hampton, he remembered the purchase he was supposed to make. Had to make. Freedah will send me back out into Atlanta to get a mannequin if I forget, he thought. I better get downtown and see if I can find a used store window dummy or something else.

John looked around as he waited at a red light in the center of town, but there was nothing. A restaurant. A book store. Driving a little farther, he saw a sign for an old theater and just down the block, a shop for theater props and costumes. That's more like it. Maybe they will have something. Something cheap, he thought.

He pulled into the parking lot behind the store, got out and walked to the building. The sign there read "Open: 11 a.m. to 6 p.m." He had ten minutes.

He opened the green, heavy, wooden back door to the sound of chimes playing "The Anvil Chorus." Okay...he thought, then called out, "Hello? Anybody here?"

"Just me." A small wiry man with thin, light reddish-brown hair and a mustache walked toward him. "What can I do for you?"

"I need a mannequin, a woman mannequin."

The small man eyed him, seemingly looking right through him. "Oh, really? What for? You own a store?"

"Yes. Well, yes. Yes, I need it for a window display. I'm John. I mean Jack."

"Glad to meet you, Jack. I'm Ralph, otherwise known as "The Great Reynard, Hypnotist Extraordinaire" on the boards, but you can call me Reynard. I might have something for you. They're all back here."

Leading him to the rear of the store, Reynard took out a key from his pocket, unlocked the door to another room and turned on the light. Propped against the wall on the left was a stack of figures that looked like ordinary store dummies, but the rest of the room was full of dozens of theater prop mannequins. "Come over here, Jack, these are the old ones," explained Reynard, "and most are made of wood. Some of the costumes are from plays you may even know."

John didn't recognize any, but said, "Well, let's take a look."

It didn't seem as if the room was full of a hundred figurines. He saw only one of them, a brunette, tall, willowy, of course, and dressed in gauzy mauve skirt and blouse. With it, she wore small, dark red, beaded jewelry, odd and old appearing. A strange feeling ran through John, as if he had known her from somewhere. That's too weird, he thought. Out loud he said, "This is the one I want."

"You sure?" asked the shopkeeper, his eyes going way into Jack's eyes. "I don't know where this one came from, but she's a beauty. Special. One of a kind. You positive you need it for a window display?"

John couldn't tell him that Freedah insisted he have a parole officer. He tried to act nonchalant as he asked, "How much?"

"Two hundred."

"What? I can get plastic for $35!"

"Fine. This one is two hundred. And she comes with a case. She folds up into a very tidy package."

John slowly pulled out his wallet. "Well, all right, I don't have time tonight to look any more. Here you go," he said, handing him ten twenties.

Reynard quickly moved the wooden arms, legs and hips and placed the figure into a small canvas case. "You made a good buy, Jack," Reynard said softly. "I wish you luck. Now I've got to close. I have a performance tonight, like I told you, ' I'm The Great Reynard.' "

"What do you do?"

"Magic, Jack, magic."

*******

In fifteen minutes, John was at the Hampton. He parked, took out his overnight case, laptop, and the wheeled canvas bag holding his new wooden figure. As he trundled them inside, he thought how business-like this looked. Louise had folded only at the waist and had to be carried in a large, black garbage bag. When the desk clerk asked him for his reservation, he started to say John Dunlap then stopped, "Jack Dunlap. Do you need my reservation number?"

"No, that's okay. We have you under the name John."

"It should say Jack," he said firmly. With a smile he took his card, cases, found the elevator and his room.

"Motel rooms sure look alike, every night," he said out loud, "but at least I have a new companion. Come on, Louise #2. Shall I call you Lou #2?"

He carefully lifted the collapsed wooden figure out of the case and found it easy to unfold. She was wonderfully made, he observed, quite amazed. Her ankles and hands had tiny screws that allowed her feet to move independently of her legs and arms; her knees moved like real joints, and so did her hips, shoulders and elbows. Everything! "You're a miracle," he said to her. "You're almost human. A wooden doll, but life size."

He looked at her face again. That was what had drawn him to her. She seemed alive, and beautiful beyond what he had realized back in the theater shop. She had real hair, brunette with a touch of auburn, and a permanent smile on her lovely face. Her "skin" was the color of light ash. He was dumbfounded and felt overwhelmed with his purchase.

Placing her carefully in the large motel chair, Jack sat down on the edge of the bed and said, "I guess you're no Louise, no Lou #2. You're a Dolly. My Dolly. Hello, Dolly, I'm Jack. We're going to be friends."

He put a Do Not Disturb sign on the doorknob, went to a small restaurant next door for a quick supper, then hurried back to his room. Dolly was safe, just where he left her. Tired, he showered and fell into bed, nodding toward the mannequin, "G'nite, Dolly," and closed his eyes. She smiled.

He did not waken until almost morning. A soft voice was saying, "Hello, Jack," and a warm arm reached around him. Startled, he fell out of bed, which completely woke him up. Jack looked back at the bed - nobody. He got up and walked around to the other side. Nothing. He glanced over at the chair. She wasn't there. But there were two coffee cups on the round table near the window. One had lipstick on the edge. This is nuts, he thought. Feeling foolish and a little angry, he opened the closet door. Dolly wasn't there. He sat back down on the edge of the empty bed. Come on, Jack, he thought, it's six a.m. You're Jack Dunlap. You're fifty-one years old, live in a small town near Atlanta, and you're in a Hampton motel room in Asheville, North Carolina. That much I'm sure of...but...all of this? No way! Maybe a cup of coffee and seeing some real people will help.

When he entered the motel dining room, he tripped and almost fell down, for over by the window at a small table he saw Dolly sitting with a man who was tall, well dressed and good looking. He was talking loudly about hog futures. Dolly saw Jack and waved to him, winking.

Jack walked a little closer, stopped, then turned on his heel, and ran out. Angrily, he punched the elevator button. He would make coffee in his room and leave. But when he opened the door and glanced in, there on the bed was Dolly. Wooden Dolly. He grabbed her, folded her up and stuffed her into her case. "Now, stay there, dammit!"
Jack drank some very bad coffee, e-mailed regrets to the Asheville appointments and packed his things. As he leaned over and picked up the Dolly case, he thought he heard a giggle.

"That's not funny, Dolly, be quiet." In the car, he left her in the case, even though he thought he heard muffled entreaties. It was a long, fast ride home.

*******

Jack never came home on a Tuesday evening. Freedah was sitting by the edge of the pool, talking with George the gardener. Startled, she jumped up hurriedly, knocking over the chair. "John. John, dear! This isn't like you! Whatever is the matter? Why are you here? Is something wrong?"

"No, nothing's wrong. I had a couple of canceled appointments, so I'll be going to Sarasota tomorrow."

"Well, I'll be right in. Just let me finish talking with Jorge about the begonias."

Jack eyed the two drinks on the patio table. Two drinks with umbrellas? "Jorge? You mean George?"

"Jorge, John, he's a purebred Castile. From Spain."

Sounds like a bar of soap, he thought, purebred lazy more like it. He probably has never heard of Spain. Out loud he said, "All right. I'll go unpack."

Jack put his car in the garage, threw the Dolly case into the closet there and locked the door.

Supper was frozen pot pies. Again. Frozen green beans. Frozen brownies, mostly thawed. No umbrella drinks, he noticed.

Sleep did not come that night. Jack lay there a long time listening to Freedah. She snored, and as usual, lay there without moving.

Finally, toward morning, Jack got up, dressed and went to

the garage. He unlocked the closet door and took out the case. Dolly was easy to assemble. It seemed the limbs almost put themselves together. And there she was, Dolly. She smiled and said, "Hello, Jack. I'm glad you're back," and threw herself into his arms.

Somehow, Jack was not surprised. He grinned at her, "Come on, Dolly, let's go for a ride."

Gently he opened the passenger door. Dolly slipped in, her skirt catching on the seat just enough to slide up her leg. Jack tried not to notice, but knew he was noticing. "Wait, I need a few things."

Freedah was still asleep. She looked very brown. All that sunshine and fresh air, must be, that you get while deciding where to plant the begonias, went through his mind. He looked at her again. She was really brown. In the early morning sun, her skin looked dried out, a little wooden. "Nah, maybe it's the light," he muttered quietly.

Jack gathered up some papers, clothes, all the checkbooks, and slipped Freedah's credit cards out of her purse.

Dolly was waiting and smiling. Jack laughed out loud as he sat down behind the wheel. He started the car slowly, backed quietly out of the drive, then picked up speed as they drove quickly through the neighborhood. The highway lay just ahead.

Jack didn't notice the police car parked at the corner of the town's only four-way stop.

The driver, Charlie, glanced at his partner, "Hey, Pete, that Lexus didn't make much of a stop."

"You're right, hit the lights. Wait, no, never mind, that's just Jack Dunlap. Why's he out at sunrise?"

"I don't know. Maybe he's taking Freedah to the hospital."

"Charlie, that doesn't look like Freedah."

"I guess not."

"What a doll! Is she waving to us?" Pete waved back at Dolly.

Charlie looked after the car for a long time. He finally said, "I don't know, Pete." He smiled and said half to himself, "I'll see ya, Jack."

## Epilogue

Jack moved to Asheville and went into business with Ralph as manager for "The Amazing Reynard, Hypnotist Extraordinaire." They traveled to colleges and universities all over the Southeast.

He met and married Sally, a widow with two grown sons. She was a UNC assistant professor of theater.

Dolly stood in the lobby of Ralph and Jack's renovated theater, greeted every one with a beautiful smile and never missed a performance.

Freedah learned how to cook tamales.

## Just Ask

If you ask me to pray,
I always say yes
and remember you in church,
where God hears me clearly
and will answer more quickly.
Or, do my prayers linger there
waiting in a pew where I have knelt?
Will a custodian find them
before you do, God?

If I pray for you at home,
do my prayers fall from my lips,
slip off my chin,
bounce on my shoes
and lie covering my floors
ankle deep, wall to wall?
Dust bunnies of prayers
said for you, you and you,
just where they have dropped.

We are told to, "Just ask."

We ask, Spirit of God, here for us,
bring your celestial broom,
follow me, see me,
pick up after me.
The prayers I say,
the prayers I think.
Sweep them up
and bring them
to your Holy Self.

## Justice by Lena

She shot him four times in the head.
He wuz lying right there on the couch.
Darn dead, ol' Herman, the fool.
Now it's four counts for Lena,
murder, murder,
assault, possession.

"Jes 'cuz we wuz married, kinda,
goin' on 65 years or so, I guess.
Thought you cud fule yer Lena, huh?
Nope, not me.
I be'n peekin in the winda.
Din't see ya.
Coon't hear ya snorin.
Knowed you waren't takin no nap.
Ya war a geeeratrk geegalo
lak they sez on thet thar teevee.
Yesiree.
You gut whut wuz comin."

At 85,
'ol Herman Winslow's dead, all right.
At 79,
Lena's in the pokey for life.

## Lispeth's Birthday

"Mommy, I want a griffin for my birthday this year, okay?"

"That would be fine, Lispeth," Mommy replied. "We'll go to the pet store tomorrow after school."

"Thank you, Mommy. I am so, so excited!" said Lispeth, jumping up and down.

The next day Mommy and Lispeth hurried to the pet store.

"Hello, Mr. Pet Store man. I'm Lispeth. I'm going to be five. That's old enough to have a griffin."

Mr. Pet Store man was delighted to have such a grownup little girl want one of his griffins.

"Sure, Lispeth. Come right over here to the griffin cage," said Mr. Pet Store man. Mommy followed closely behind them.

"Oh, no!" he exclaimed, peering into the cage. "They're all gone. I forgot this is the week of the Griffin Convention. All my griffins have flown to Chicago."

Lispeth started to cry.

"Now, now, don't do that, Lispeth. How about a little puppy? Look. Down here. Freddie is wagging his tail and wants you to pick him up."

Lispeth snuggled Freddie into her arms. He licked her face. "Oh, Mommy, I want Freddie for my birthday, okay?"

"Of course, sweetie," smiled her mother. "Let's take him home and show him to your Daddy and your little brother."

115

## Not a Poem

I'm not a Poem when I walk,
no grace-filled beauty
floating by.
Not I,
I waddle.

I'm not a Poem when I talk,
Juliet-tones making
music sigh.
Not I,
I prattle.

I'm not a Poem when I sit,
elegance of posture queen,
head held high.
Not I,
I droop.

I'm not a Poem when I stand
hips and chest and toes so tall,
plumb line try.
Not I,
I stoop.

But in my head
as I lie in bed,
thoughts fly by,
and I am
a Poem.

## Not Writing

I had a second cup of tea,
read all the want ads,
took my time cleaning up the table,
looked around for something else,
anything,
whatever,
that could keep me from writing
and telling you
and the world
how my heart feels today.

## Poem House

This is not a poem, it is a house.
I build it stone by stone,
board by board, nail by nail.
Word by word.
When it is done, I move in and live there.

Each room is the size I want,
where I want,
with doors and floors and walls
where they should be, as planned.

I paint it special colors,
opalescent and gray,
accents of ruby and jade on one curved wall.
The other four are palest yellow.

Furniture is placed and re-placed.
I move a chair an eighth of an inch to the right,
back a quarter of an inch -
then throw it out the window.

It's my poem, my house.
I look around, change one pillow,
peer with half-closed eyes and like what I see.
It's my poem, my house.

I walk through once more,
smile and step outside,
turn the key in the lock
and move on to my next Poem House.

## Scents of Life

Freezing, nose-cracking air on an ice-crackling night.
Orange-peel spray shooting out on your hands.
Sun-soaked, slightly sweaty faces of children playing outdoors in summer.
May lilies-of-the-valley dripping sweetness from white bells.
A blue spruce carried in for Christmas.

Strawberry jam on a biscuit.
Wind-and-sun-dried white sheets on your bed at night.
Cherries and berries and kraut.
Lightning bolts shattering ozone into hot, rain-filled Illinois afternoons.
Hickory nuts under an autumn tree.

A mowing of hay and dust.
Maple leaves transformed into smoky scent.
Love-making, complete.
Yeast-dissolving-dough-kneading-bread-baking.
Twenty acres of dirt made by God, April-plowed.

Roses, peaches, clover and cloves.
Wet dogs.
Mud.
New-cut green grass.
Sweetness of a baby's neck.

Senses of life.

## The Eleventh McGriffin

Griffin eggs are very special. After twenty years of waiting, Mr. Edwin and Mrs. Edwiana McGriffin were sure their eleventh egg would hatch today. It was time.

Their ten offspring, Edwin I, Edwin II, Edwin III, Edwin IV, Edwin V, Edwiana 1, Edwiana 2, Edwiana 3, Edwiana 4, and Edwiana 5, peered excitedly into the huge nest holding the giant egg.

"Oh! Look! It's happening!" they all shouted together.

The shell cracked and out hopped their new baby brother. He had the proud face, beak, fierce wings and claws of an eagle, and the strong hind legs and body of a lion, complete with tail swishing in the air. He was perfect.

Except he was plaid. Black and yellow plaid in front, yellow and black plaid in the back.

"Oh, me-oh-my," cried all the Edwianas.

"Gosh," said the Edwins.

Mother McGriffin said, "Now, children, don't worry. Just take your little brother, Scotsy, outside and play with all the other griffins – the Griffs, the Griffinis, the Griffolowskis, the O'Griffs, the Griffoborskis, the Grifflesteins – all of them. Chances are no one will notice that your brother is plaid."

And no one did.

# Thickening

Thickening clouds....
   ...aaah

Thickening plot....
   ...hmmm

Thickening snow....
   ...brrrr

Thickening soup....
   ...yum

Thickening ice....
   ...whoops

Thickening waist....
   ...oops

Thickening speesh....
   ...hic

Thickening dust....
   ...'choo

Thickening smoke....
   ...cof

Thickening fog....
   ...boo

Thickening breast....
   ...         not!

## Thursday Morning Walk

I take my words for a walk each morning,
or else, my words take me.
No dog to tug and lug along
that stops by a bush,
a bush and a bush,
then stops by a bush for a pee.

No, we wander on, my words and I
with sun and sky and song.
The breeze sings me,
the sky sings me,
songs sing to me,
and the song I sing is me.

# When
*1 Corinthians 13:12*

When finally I see face to face,
what kind of face shall I see?
When this body is no longer mine,
what sort of shape will I be?

When all earthly treasures
I've polished and kept,
put away so carefully
are taken away, without any say
from an all-knowing, all-bossy she.

When you, our God,
in the blink of an eye
bring love in transfulgent light,
what will you see?
Me.

## Where Have All The Old Girls Gone?

Where are all the Shirleys?
What's happened to Marie?
Who's ever seen a Clementine,
Claudette or Maude, Penelope?

Have we lost track of Clara?
Edna, Ruby, Blanche, Louise,
Frances, Florence, Hortense, Prudence,
where, tell me please, is one of these.

Sweet Lorraine is just a song.
The wind is called Mariah.
Grace is Gracie, Catherine, Caitlyn,
an Alice now Aaliyah.

Who knows a Hazel, Laverne or Eve,
Dora or Flora, Louella, Lenore,
Opal, Ruby, Belle, Adele,
Diedre, Daphne, Gwen, Eleanor?

Janine?
      Not seen.
Fay?
      No way.
Elaine?
      In Spain.
Rose?
      Who knows.
Dawn?
      Gone.

So, it's ...
Goodbye, you old girls,
here come the new.
From Ashley to Zoe
the world is waiting for you.

# [ 2008 ]

## Again

You held my hand last night
and kept me,
        again,
from sailing off this
round world into
       who knows what,

   where
I might not be me
     or anything.

## Car Gene

Is it a rogue gene? I can't help myself. Here I am, gender female, wearing lipstick, earrings, yet I can be stopped dead in my tracks whenever the low purr of a Cadillac Catera catches my ear.

If I'm out on my morning walk and suddenly my heart skips a beat, I know it's out there. Just ahead of me, on the corner, it lurks, big motor idling, whispering its seductive, sweet murmur. I see this car is silver, but it could be blue, gold, black. It is the sound that speaks and something deep inside, reverberates, responds. I'm captive.

This shouldn't happen. It ought to be the scent of a French perfume...Nope. Pretty shoes...Ho-hum. A Gucci bag...No thanks. A handsome, dark-eyed man...No way. The latest dresses...Yawn, yawn. Flower-festooned, wide brimmed hats...Boring. Take me to the Mall to shop I can hardly wait to leave.

But. The annual new car show? The latest Lexus? Cadillac? An Audi? A BMW? Mercedes-Benz? Nirvana on earth.

Our twice-a-year visit to the car dealership for an oil change in our old anthracite-blue station wagon can become an out-of-body experience. While sitting there docilely, folded hands in my lap, I am transported into the new car show room.

I don't remember walking in there. On its own, I see my right hand has reached out and is lightly caressing the side of a pearl gray Audi, the highest priced car in sight. Next, I find my head is through the open front window and I am breathing in, fiercely, deeply, the exquisite fragrance of a luxury automobile.

Are my feet on the floor? I don't know and I don't care. I am almost overcome.

"May I help you?" It is the voice of the solicitous salesman.

"Oh yes," I reply, holding on to the door frame. "Why yes," I mumble, "tell me, why does the front seat have those extra leather inserts?" Pretty poor, Ruth, I say to myself, but it's all I can think of.

"Good question, ma'am, it's for looks. Here, why don't you get in and see how comfortable it is."

Oh yes, yes, I'm thinking. He opens the door and I slide onto the buttery leather seat, slowly bringing my damp fingers around the smooth solid wheel. Careful, don't grip too tightly. I place my right foot on the gas pedal. "Oh my, young man, this is very comfortable."

I sit there and see myself speeding down a lightly traveled highway. "How does it drive?" I ask. I don't hear his answer, I know how it drives. I can't tell him I am passionately in love with this engineering marvel. I hope he can't hear the pounding of my heart.

"Oh, yes, ma'am."

What is he saying? What have I asked? Gently, I touch the dash and run my hand over the sleek gearshift. I smile and get out very slowly. "You're right. It's a fine car. Thank you very much."

I look for the service waiting area and slowly make my way back there. My husband is paying the bill. He knows where I have been, and by my happy face that I've been looking at expensive new cars. He doesn't mind. I can't help it.

## It Is the Season

Why is it? The darkest time of the year. The shortest days. Flu bugs and sniffles abound. And yet, we celebrate. We have parties. We wear spangley clothes and bring out our lightly used Christmas sweaters.

Once a year, we get in touch with friends and relatives to catch up on what has happened in the last twelve months. We mail cards and notes. E-mail. Phone.

And we decorate. Wreaths, ribbons, bells make festive our houses, yards, cars, dogs, golf carts and mailboxes. There is an eight-foot inflated snowman in someone's front yard, a tasseled red hat on the stone flutist in another garden.

Lights are everywhere. Simple, lit candles shine from front windows. Decorated trees sparkle in neighborhood living rooms and cold yards. White lights on wire mesh form a circular tree, a nativity scene, reindeer, or a Santa Claus. Palm trees and bare tree branches twinkle. Fake icicles hang from eaves. Lit luminaria and candy canes line sidewalk entrances.

We are no different at our house, we celebrate. The day after Thanksgiving, boxes of decorations are brought out. The three-inch, be-ribboned Christmas tree goes on top of our mailbox. An old magazine cover with "Merry Christmas, God" is pasted on a front hall mirror.

We place a potpourri of mementos and trinkets in all the rooms. Bells of glass, yarn and brass. Windowsills are filled with ceramic, crocheted and woven angels, infant booties. A little red elf; a one-inch, big-eared deer head in a Santa hat; small scarlet boxes with pasted-on hearts; a painted, winged-bird tree ornament; one very large foam strawberry and a pair of tiny, red doll mittens. All are little treasures that have been part of us for years.

Live plants are tied with ribbons. A white teapot wears a crimson bow. Christmas stockings are taped on mirrors; large, starched, white crocheted snowflakes are pasted onto sunroom windows; multi-colored, round tree ornaments dangle on colored ribbons.

Red and green African candles rest on a high shelf. Our five-inch Russian doll stands alone on the coffee table surveying the room with painted, all-seeing eyes.

Pictures of sailboats have been taken down from living room walls and up go artworks of Joseph, Mary and Jesus; *Joy*, borders a black silhouette of a dancer; *Acclamation*, on a musical staff; Hebrew *Jesu*; reflective *Beatitudes*.

Silver garlands surround the Advent wreath; nearby are two crèches with wise men riding along on camels. Shepherds wait in a manger. A golden star hangs in an open wall.

Each year we stop. We celebrate, decorating our house and lives during these dark December days. It brings us memories, joy and again, the renewing love of Christmas

# Limbo

The Pope in his papal wisdom has declared
that babies born without breath,
in other words, dead,
and those never baptized,
now have hope because there is a new study.

Though, remember, they for centuries have enjoyed
an eternal state of perfect natural happiness,
    Limbo.

Again, nota bene,
Limbo means without being in communion with
    God.

Nothing like being without God
    for perfect happiness.

# The Doctors

Today I'll see some doctors
at ten and two and three.
They need to check my eyeballs,
my liver and my knee.

The first doc eyes my eyeballs,
the next one pokes at me.
My kneebone bends like always -
I'm good for eighty-three.

Tomorrow is the dentist.
She peers into my teeth.
It's time for many X-rays,
some fungus underneath?

Thursday is the heart guru.
Friday, lungs and feet and skin.
Many tests and many probes
to see my inner in.

They rule out death and dying
and send me to the nurse.
She schedules days of rechecks.
My nothing might get worse.

# [ 2009 ]

## Cyrus Davis

Cyrus Davis was my maternal grandfather. He was over six feet tall, bony, and had a circular layer of thin white hair around his otherwise bald head. I can't remember ever hearing him laugh or seeing him smile. He chewed tobacco. Indoors, he spat the juice at an old, smelly metal spittoon. He and my grandmother, Clara, lived on 120 acres in northeastern Indiana in an old two-story wooden house. He farmed, not very successfully.

When our family visited there on a Sunday, some of our eight cousins and aunts and uncles might be there. Grandma Davis made dinner on her black, wood-burning stove, fixing a chicken or two that had been scratching around the chicken yard just a few hours before. She always served mounds of creamy white mashed potatoes, gravy, biscuits, green beans cooked for at least an hour with a small piece of home-cured bacon, platters of sliced garden tomatoes, and fruit pies for dessert.

After dinner was over, the women, including my oldest cousin, Louise, stayed indoors to clean up the kitchen and then sat and visited, often sewing. As the only other girl, and much younger, I went along to play with my two brothers and any of the younger boys who were there.

The men immediately went outdoors to talk farming. My three uncles had big farms and helped Grandpa with chores when they were there. The older boy cousins often went to the shed behind the garage, probably to play cards, which wasn't permitted on Sundays.

We children ran outside to walk down the garden rows looking for strawberries or radishes to eat, wander back to the mulberry tree to see if those purple staining berries were ripe, or visit the outhouse near there. We chased the chickens, lay on the grass, watching clouds puff by in the blue sky, and gazed out over nearby fields of growing corn, wheat or potatoes. To us it was flat land; Grandpa Davis used to say, correcting us, "No, there was a rise of at least a foot or two in the next mile."

We took turns playing in Grandpa's model T, beeping the horn and trying to move the little gearshift on the wheel. We made sure we stayed out of his way. He normally didn't speak to any of us unless we did something he didn't like. When he had had enough of talking with the men, he took his rocker from the porch and placed it under one of three big trees in the front yard. There he sat by himself, chewed and spat, silently watching the occasional car that passed by on the paved county road.

Once in a while, we youngsters were allowed in the closed off front parlor. This room had windows with side panels of small, colored glass panes. It all seemed very elegant to me. There was a real rug, an antique stiff settee we were not allowed to sit on, some wooden chairs, a curved small table or so, and best of all, an old Victrola. We wound it up, put on one of the few recorded cylinders and listened to our favorite, "Barney Google." We sang loudly along with the quavering male voice.

Soon we were sent back outside to play for as long as we could, for dusk came too soon. We took turns being "It," placing our head against one of those big trees, and with eyes closed, counted off for Hide-and-Seek. We chased fireflies as darkness came. Then, goodbyes and the long drive home.

I sometimes think of Grandpa Davis this time of year. Daylight Savings time had not yet been enacted into law in Indiana, but I doubt he would have paid any attention anyway. He farmed according to "God's time," as he called it. When dawn came, he got up. When the noon sun was straight overhead, he ate dinner. When he got tired in the afternoon, he quit.

Living by when Congress says six a.m. or six p.m. should arrive in March or April or October or November would have been sheer foolishness to him.

Maybe it still is. This year with the time change beginning three weeks earlier, we no longer wake when the sun hits our pillow. No, it's still night when alarms ring to start us on our day. It seems the whole country is late, grumpy, rushed, tired. I know I am.

Where's all the extra time we were supposed to gain with Daylight Savings coming in early March instead of early April?

I don't know.

We had lots of time when we were kids.

Sometimes I think of those days and wish I were back again in the early evening quiet of an Indiana farm with my cousins, playing Hide-and-Seek and chasing fireflies.

Poems and Stories Previously Published

*National Catholic Reporter:* A Saint in Training, I Did Not Believe, Lunch At the Club, When. *Sun City Hilton Head SunSations:* Good Morning. *Everything Under the Sun* (Catawba Press, 2008): A Certitude, A Definition of God, A Pickle, Brontosaurus Lane, Cry, Dolly, February 9, Genealogy 101, I Hadn't Planned To Love You, I'm Glad I Kissed Each Flower, Joy, Mr. and Mrs. Bentover, No Empty Attics, October, Summer Vacation As Remembered by Joe, The Best Love, When, When You Grow Old. *The Hilton Head Island Packet/Bluffton:* 897- , Just Ask, No Empty Attics, Not Writing, Seasons Greetings, The Doctors, Thickening, Thursday Morning Walk, When you Grow Old, Where Have All the Old Girls Gone.